To
_____

From
_____

PRELUDE

In the stillness of the soul, where words often fail,
Prayer rises—a whisper, a cry, a song without veil.
It bridges the heavens, a sacred thread,
Binding our hearts to the One who bled.

Through valleys deep and mountains high,
It lifts our spirits, it draws us nigh.
A voice in the silence, a hand in the dark,
A flame rekindled, a heavenly spark.

For in prayer, we find strength anew,
The promises of God, steadfast and true.
Each word we offer, each sigh, each plea,
Reaches the heart of eternity.

So enter this journey, a life of prayer,
A gift from the Father beyond compare.
Speak boldly, seek deeply, trust and believe,
In His presence, all things you'll receive.

> "Prayer is not a whisper into the void; it is the lifeline to the Creator, the channel through which mountains are moved, hearts are healed, and impossible becomes possible."

The Power of Prayer

"Prayer is not a burden or an obligation—it is the most precious gift."

Dr. Letitia McPherson

Therefore, I say unto you, what things soever ye desire, when ye pray, believe that ye receive them, and ye shall have them.

Mark 11:24

by God's Grace i Stand
PUBLISHER

The Power of Prayer

Copyright © 2025 by Dr. Letitia McPherson
All rights reserved.

No part of this publication may be reproduced, distributed, or transmitted in any form or by any means, including photocopying, recording, or other electronic or mechanical methods, without the prior written permission of the publisher, except in the case of brief quotations embodied in critical reviews and certain other noncommercial uses permitted by copyright law.

Scripture quotations are taken from the KJV and the NIV Translation * of the Bible, unless otherwise noted, and are used by permission. All rights reserved.

For permission requests, write to the publisher at:
Dr. Letitia McPherson
bishopmcpherson@gmail.com
based in North York, Ontario Canada

978-1-990266-70-6

Printed in the USA by Amazon

Other Books by Dr. Letitia McPherson

The Power of Prayer

The Power Series:

The Power of Forgiveness

The Power of Faith

The Power of Prayer

The Power of Worship

The Power of Grace

From the Mouth of the Prophet

Facing the Storms of Life

Walking Through the Valley

The Potter, The Clay, the Process

"Your prayers may rise from brokenness, but they carry the power to reach the heavens.

By choosing faith over doubt, you transform desperation into strength, and whispers into a profound testimony of divine grace."

Dr. Letitia McPherson

Table of Contents

Dedication	1
Preface	3
Introduction	7
Chapter 1: Understanding the Power of Prayer	11
Chapter 2: Faith that Moves the Fog	17
Chapter 3: Building a Prayer Habit	23
Chapter 4: The Holy Spirit and Prayer	29
Chapter 5: Trials, Tribulations, and Triumph	37
Chapter 6: Unleashing Heaven's Power	43
Chapter 7: Persistent Prayer	53
Chapter 8: Practical Prayers for Everyday Life	61
Chapter 9: Prayer as Active Ministry	69

Chapter 10: Living a Life of Prayer	77
Conclusion	85
A Prayer About Prayer	89

Dedication

This book is lovingly dedicated to my prayer partners and intercessors, the silent heroes who labor in the secret place, standing in the gap for others with unwavering faith.

To those who have prayed with me, for me, and alongside me, your dedication and persistence have been a source of strength, encouragement, and divine connection. There were times when I was unable to pray for myself, when my strength was gone, and my heart was heavy. Had it not been for your faithful prayers, I would not have been able to persevere. You have taught me the beauty of intercession and the power of unity in prayer. You have reminded me that no burden is too great, no valley too deep, when carried together before the throne of grace.

May this book serve as a tribute to your faithfulness and a reminder that every whispered petition, every fervent cry, and every quiet moment of intercession reaches the heart of God.

The Power of Prayer

Together, we have witnessed His miracles, His grace, and His unfailing love.

With gratitude and love,
Dr. Letitia McPherson

Preface

Prayer has been my unwavering companion throughout every season of my life. It has carried me through moments of uncontainable joy, as well as through valleys of deep sorrow. Whether in the quiet whispers of thanksgiving or the desperate cries for deliverance, prayer has been the golden thread weaving the fabric of my life together. In prayer, I have found the safest refuge—a place where my heart can lay bare, vulnerable, and unfiltered before the One who knows me fully. Time after time, I have witnessed the remarkable ways God responds—sometimes through miraculous interventions and other times through gentle, quiet transformations visible only to the eyes of faith.

This book was not merely written; it was birthed through those sacred moments of communion with God. It is not a mere guide or collection of teachings; it is my testimony. It stands as a declaration of the power of a God who hears, sees, and acts in response to the prayers of His people. Over the years, I have faced trials that threatened to overwhelm me—physical illnesses, personal losses, seasons of waiting, and moments of uncertainty. Yet, prayer was my anchor. It wasn't always easy. There were times I struggled to find the words to pray or even the strength to try. Yet, even in those moments of silence, God met me with His boundless grace and faithfulness.

As you turn these pages, my hope and prayer for you are simple: that you will discover the beauty, power, and transformative nature of prayer. This book is for the weary soul who has wondered if their prayers are heard, for the believer who yearns to see God move in mighty ways, and for the seeker who desires a deeper connection with the Creator. It is for the one who waits, the one who doubts, and the one who perseveres.

Prayer is not a burden or an obligation—it is the most precious gift. It is an open invitation to commune with the Creator of the heavens and the earth, to lay down our burdens at His feet, and to partner with Him in His redemptive work in the world. Prayer is where heaven touches earth and where the miraculous becomes possible.

As you read, may your heart be stirred to pray with boldness, persistence, and unshakable faith. May you come to know, as I have, that the God who holds the universe is the same God who holds you tenderly in His hands. Together, let us embark on this journey of prayer, discovering the fullness of His presence and the extraordinary ways He works through our prayers.

Introduction

Prayer is a mystery and a marvel, a gift given to us by a God who not only listens but also invites us into His very heart. It is not merely a spiritual discipline or a ritual; it is the lifeline of our relationship with the Almighty. Through prayer, we are drawn into the holy presence of the One who spoke the universe into being. We are given the privilege of partnering with Him in shaping the world and changing lives, starting with our own.

In this book, we will explore the depths and dimensions of prayer—its power, its purpose, and its profound impact. Prayer is more than just asking for God's intervention in times of need; it is about aligning our hearts with His, seeking His will, and learning to trust in His timing. Scripture reminds us of the incredible potential of prayer: "The prayer of a righteous person is powerful and effective" (James 5:16). From the intercession of Moses on behalf of Israel to the prayers of Hannah, Elijah, and even Jesus Himself, the Bible overflows with testimonies of how prayer has changed the course of history.

In my own life, I have witnessed the undeniable power of prayer. I have seen God's hand move mountains of impossibility, soften hearts of stone, and provide peace in storms that threatened to consume me. Prayer has been my constant—through health challenges, personal trials, and moments of uncertainty. Each prayer, whether uttered in desperation or whispered in faith, has been a step closer to His heart. And each answered prayer, whether immediate or delayed, has been a testament to His unchanging love and faithfulness.

This book is an invitation. It is an invitation to those who feel unworthy to pray, to those who are weary of waiting for answers, and to those who simply long to draw closer to God. Together, we will explore practical ways to cultivate a deeper prayer life, drawing inspiration from biblical examples and personal stories of God's faithfulness. We will look at the various types of prayer—adoration, confession, thanksgiving, and supplication—and how each connects us to God in unique and powerful ways.

Jesus Himself taught us the importance of prayer. When His disciples asked Him, "Lord, teach us to pray," He gave them what we now call the Lord's Prayer (Luke 11:1-4). In this prayer, Jesus revealed the heart of true communion with

God—a prayer that acknowledges His holiness, submits to His will, seeks His provision, and extends His grace.

As you read, my prayer for you is that you will be inspired to embrace prayer not as a last resort but as your first response. May you approach God with confidence, knowing that He delights in your prayers (Proverbs 15:8). May this journey draw you closer to His heart, transforming not only your circumstances but also your soul. For the God who calls us to pray is faithful, and He is able to do "immeasurably more than all we ask or imagine, according to His power that is at work within us" (Ephesians 3:20).

Let us embark together on this sacred journey of prayer, trusting that the One who invites us into His presence will meet us there with open arms.

CHAPTER 1

Understanding the Power of Prayer

Prayer is not merely a religious practice; it is a gateway to communion with God and a source of divine power. Let me tell you about George Mueller. Have you heard of him? He's an incredible example of someone who lived by prayer. Mueller never asked anyone for money to support his ministry for orphans; he only prayed. Time after time, God provided exactly what was needed. One story that always amazes me is when Mueller had to travel to Quebec and encountered a dense fog. He told the ship's captain, "My eye is not on the density of the fog, but on the living God who controls every circumstance of life." And you know what? After he prayed, the fog lifted, and he made it to his engagement on time.

Prayer connects us to a God who is greater than our challenges. This is what I want you to take to heart as we journey through this book. But let me ask you: what does prayer mean to you? Is it a ritual, a habit, or an act of desperation? For many people, prayer can feel like throwing words into the void, unsure if God is even listening. I've been there too. Yet, I've discovered that prayer is so much more than a one-way conversation—it's a dialogue with the Creator of the universe who loves us deeply.

I remember the first time I truly experienced the power of prayer. It wasn't during a peaceful moment or in a quiet chapel. It was in a moment of absolute chaos. I had just received devastating news, and my world felt like it was crumbling. I dropped to my knees, tears streaming down my face, and simply cried out, "Lord, I don't know what to do." In that raw, vulnerable moment, I felt an overwhelming peace wash over me—a peace that didn't make sense given the circumstances. That's when I knew: God hears. He listens. And He answers.

Prayer is not about using fancy words or following a strict formula. It's about being honest with God. Sometimes, my prayers are as simple as, "Help me, Lord." Other times, they're filled with gratitude or specific requests. The beauty of prayer is that God meets us where we are. He doesn't require perfection; He desires our hearts.

The Bible is full of examples of the power of

prayer. Think of Elijah, who prayed for rain after three years of drought, and God answered (1 Kings 18:41-45). Or consider Hannah, who prayed fervently for a child, and God blessed her with Samuel (1 Samuel 1:10-20). These stories remind us that prayer is powerful because it connects us to a powerful God.

But why does prayer matter? Isn't God going to do what He's going to do anyway? This is a question I've heard many times, and it's a valid one. The truth is, prayer isn't about changing God's mind; it's about aligning our hearts with His will. When we pray, we invite God to work in our lives and circumstances. We acknowledge our dependence on Him and open ourselves to His guidance.

Let me share a personal example. A few years ago, I was facing a decision that felt impossible. I had two paths before me, and both seemed equally daunting. I prayed every day for clarity, pouring out my fears and frustrations to God. At first, I didn't hear anything. It felt like God was silent, and I began to doubt whether my prayers were making a difference. But as I continued to pray, something began to change—not in my circumstances, but in me. I felt a growing sense of peace about one of the options, and eventually, doors began to open in that direction. Looking back, I can see how God was guiding me all along, even when I couldn't see it in the moment.

This is the power of prayer: it transforms us. It gives us the courage to face challenges, the wisdom to make decisions, and the peace to trust God's plan. As Philippians 4:6-7 says, "Do not be anxious about anything, but in every situation, by prayer and petition, with thanksgiving, present your requests to God. And the peace of God, which transcends all understanding, will guard your hearts and your minds in Christ Jesus."

So, how can we make prayer a central part of our lives? Start where you are. You don't need to pray for hours or use elaborate language. Simply talk to God as you would a close friend. Share your joys, your fears, your hopes, and your struggles. And don't forget to listen. Prayer is not just about speaking; it's also about hearing God's voice. Sometimes, His answer comes through Scripture, a gentle nudge in your spirit, or the wise counsel of a friend.

As we move through this book, my prayer is that you will not only understand the power of prayer but also experience it for yourself. Whether you're facing a dense fog like George Mueller or a personal crisis, know that prayer connects you to a God who loves you and is ready to move mountains on your behalf.

Chapter 2

Faith that Moves the Fog

Faith is the foundation of powerful prayer. Let me ask you—when you pray, do you truly believe God will answer? George Mueller did. His simple yet confident prayers continue to inspire me to trust God with unwavering faith. Imagine facing dense fog on a ship, knowing your journey depends on visibility, and yet declaring boldly, "My eye is not on the density of the fog, but on the living God who controls every circumstance of life." That's the kind of faith Mueller had, and it's the kind of faith we're called to develop.

The Power of Prayer

I've experienced moments in my life when prayer felt like the only lifeline. Have you been there too? There was a time when I was overwhelmed with decisions, doubts, and fears. It felt like the world was closing in on me, much like that fog that surrounded Mueller. In those moments, I learned something profound: faith doesn't deny the reality of the fog; it simply chooses to see beyond it. Faith fixes its eyes on God, not the problem.

The Bible gives us so many examples of faith that moved mountains—or fog. Think of Abraham, who believed God's promise even when it seemed impossible (Romans 4:20-21). Or Peter, who stepped out of the boat and walked on water toward Jesus (Matthew 14:29). These stories remind us that faith isn't about having all the answers; it's about trusting the One who does.

But let's be honest—faith isn't always easy. Sometimes, our circumstances scream louder than our prayers. In those moments, it's tempting to doubt whether God is listening or whether our prayers even matter. I've wrestled with these doubts too. Yet, every time I've chosen to trust God despite the doubts, I've seen Him move in ways I never expected.

One of the lessons I've learned is that faith grows through practice. It's like a muscle that strengthens with use. Start small. Pray for something specific, even if it seems minor. When you see God answer that prayer, your faith will grow. Then, pray for something bigger. Over time, you'll develop the kind of faith that can face dense fog—or any obstacle—and say, "My eye is on God."

Another key to building faith is meditating on God's Word. Romans 10:17 says, "Faith comes by hearing, and hearing by the word of God." When we fill our minds with Scripture, we remind ourselves of God's promises and character. During one particularly challenging season, I clung to Proverbs 3:5-6: "Trust in the Lord with all your heart and lean not on your own understanding; in all your ways acknowledge Him, and He shall direct your paths." Those words became my anchor, steadying me when everything else felt uncertain.

Faith also requires action. James 2:26 tells us that "faith without works is dead." True faith isn't passive; it moves us to step out, even when we can't see the full picture. Remember when Peter stepped out of the boat? He didn't wait for the water to solidify beneath his feet; he trusted Jesus and took the first step. What step of faith is God asking you to take today? Maybe it's forgiving someone who hurt you, pursuing a dream He's placed on your heart, or simply trusting Him with an unresolved situation. Whatever it is, take that step. Faith grows as we walk in obedience.

Let me share one more personal story. A few years ago, I faced a situation that seemed impossible. I had prayed and prayed, but nothing seemed to change. Honestly, I was ready to give up. But then I felt a gentle nudge in my spirit—a reminder that faith doesn't give up. So, I prayed one more time, this time surrendering the situation completely to God. And you know what? He came through. Not in the way I expected, but in a way that was far better than I could have imagined. That experience taught me that faith isn't about getting the outcome we want; it's about trusting God's plan, even when it doesn't make sense.

As we reflect on faith that moves the fog, let's remember this: faith is not about the absence of doubt; it's about choosing to trust God in the midst of doubt. It's about fixing our eyes on Him, not the fog. When we do, we'll see Him move mountains, part seas, and lift the fog in ways that only He can.

What about you? What is the fog in your life right now? Is it a financial struggle, a broken relationship, a health issue, or uncertainty about the future? Whatever it is, I encourage you to take it to God in prayer. Believe that He hears you, trust that He is working, and watch as He moves the fog one step at a time.

Chapter 3

Building a Prayer Habit

Can I share something personal? A few years ago, I started using a prayer journal, and it completely changed my prayer life. At first, I thought it was just another thing to keep track of, but it turned into a treasure. Writing down my prayers and then crossing them off when God answered was like watching Him move in real-time. Do you keep a prayer journal? If not, I encourage you to start. It's one of the best ways to stay consistent and intentional in your prayer life.

The Power of Prayer

Let's be honest—building a habit of prayer isn't always easy. Life gets busy. We have work, family, responsibilities, and distractions that compete for our attention. Some days, it feels like there just isn't enough time to sit down and pray. I've been there too. But here's what I've learned: prayer doesn't require perfection, just intention. It's not about how long you pray or finding the perfect words; it's about showing up consistently and connecting with God.

Think about it this way: imagine you have a close friend. If you only talked to them once in a while or when you needed something, that friendship wouldn't grow very deep, would it? The same is true with God. Prayer is our conversation with Him, and the more time we spend talking to Him, the deeper our relationship becomes.

One of the best ways to make prayer a habit is

to set aside a specific time each day. For me, mornings work best. Before the chaos of the day begins, I grab my prayer journal, a cup of coffee, and sit in a quiet corner. It's my time to reflect, pour out my heart, and listen for God's voice. What about you? Are you a morning person, or do evenings work better for you? The key is finding a time that works for you and sticking with it. But let's get practical. What do you do when you sit down to pray? Some people feel stuck because they don't know where to start. If that's you, here are a few suggestions to get you going

Start with Gratitude: Begin by thanking God for His blessings. Gratitude shifts your focus from your problems to His goodness.

Write It Down: Use a prayer journal to list your prayer requests. Writing things down helps you stay focused and gives you a record of God's faithfulness.

Pray Scripture: Open your Bible and turn a verse into a prayer. For example, Psalm 23:1 says, "The Lord is my shepherd; I shall not want." You could pray, "Lord, thank You for being my shepherd. I trust You to provide everything I need.

Be Honest: Don't feel like you have to hide your doubts, fears, or struggles. God already knows what's on your heart, so talk to Him about it.

Listen: Prayer isn't just about talking; it's also about listening. Sit quietly and ask God to speak to your heart. Sometimes, His answers come through Scripture, a song, or a gentle nudge in your spirit.

Another thing that has helped me stay consistent in prayer is creating a prayer list. I divide my journal into sections: personal needs, family and friends, church and ministry, and the world. Each day, I focus on a different section. It keeps my prayers organized and ensures that nothing gets overlooked.

Over time, you'll notice something amazing happening. As you pray regularly, you'll become more attuned to God's voice. You'll start seeing His hand at work in your life in ways you never noticed before. And when you look back at your journal and see all the prayers He's answered, your faith will grow. I want to encourage you: if you miss a day—or even a week—don't let guilt keep you from starting again. Building a prayer habit is like learning to ride a bike. You might stumble or fall at first, but the more you practice, the steadier you'll become. The important thing is to keep showing up.

One final thought: prayer doesn't have to be confined to a specific time or place. While having a

The Power of Prayer

dedicated prayer time is important, don't underestimate the power of short, spontaneous prayers throughout the day. Whether you're driving, washing dishes, or taking a walk, those little moments of connection with God can make a big difference. So, let's commit to making prayer a priority. Let's carve out time to meet with God, build a habit of journaling, and keep the lines of communication open. I promise you, the more you invest in your prayer life, the more you'll experience the peace, guidance, and power of God in your everyday life.

Chapter 4

The Holy Spirit and Prayer

The Holy Spirit is such a gift, isn't He? There have been moments in my life when I felt completely lost in prayer, unsure of what to say or how to even begin. But in those moments, the Holy Spirit stepped in, interceding for me with a depth of understanding that goes beyond words. Romans 8:26 beautifully captures this: "In the same way, the Spirit helps us in our weakness. We do not know what we ought to pray for, but the Spirit Himself intercedes for us through wordless groans." Isn't that comforting? Even when we can't articulate our thoughts or feelings, the Holy Spirit translates them into prayers that align perfectly with God's will.

I remember one particularly difficult season when I didn't have the words to pray. My heart was so heavy that all I could do was sit quietly before the Lord. And yet, in that stillness, I could sense the Holy Spirit at work, bringing my unspoken needs before God. It was a humbling reminder that prayer isn't about our eloquence; it's about our dependence on Him.

Mark 1:8 says, "I indeed baptized you with water, but He will baptize you with the Holy Spirit." This baptism of the Holy Spirit empowers us in ways we can't imagine. Acts 1:8 takes it further: "But you will receive power when the Holy Spirit comes upon you; and you will be My witnesses in Jerusalem, and in all Judea and Samaria, and to the ends of the earth." This verse reminds us that the

Holy Spirit is not just a Comforter but also a source of power, enabling us to live boldly for Christ and to pray with authority.

Have you ever experienced the Holy Spirit guiding your prayers? For me, it often happens when I least expect it. I'll be praying for someone or a specific situation, and suddenly, a new thought or direction will come to mind—something I hadn't considered before. I've come to recognize this as the Holy Spirit's prompting. Sometimes, it's a nudge to pray for protection over someone, other times it's to pray for peace, healing, or clarity. The more we yield to the Spirit, the more we'll see His guidance in our prayer lives.

Another way the Holy Spirit helps us is by revealing Scripture that speaks directly to our circumstances. Have you ever been in prayer and had a Bible verse come to mind that perfectly addresses your need or concern? That's the Holy Spirit at work, bringing God's Word to life and reminding us of His promises. John 14:26 says, "But the Advocate, the Holy Spirit, whom the Father will send in My name, will teach you all things and will remind you of everything I have said to you." The Holy Spirit connects us to God's truth, giving us confidence as we pray.

One of the most powerful lessons I've learned is that the Holy Spirit doesn't just help us pray for ourselves; He also empowers us to intercede for others. There was a time when a close friend of mine was going through a crisis. I didn't know all the details, but I felt a strong urge to pray for her. As I prayed, I asked the Holy Spirit to guide my words. Later, when we spoke, she told me that the exact moment I had been praying was when she felt an overwhelming sense of peace and hope. That experience reminded me of the incredible privilege we have to partner with the Holy Spirit in prayer.

So how can we make room for the Holy Spirit in our prayer lives? Here are a few practical steps:

1. **Invite Him In:**

Begin your prayer time by asking the Holy Spirit to lead and guide you. A simple prayer like, "Holy Spirit, I invite You to speak to my heart and guide my prayers," can make all the difference.

2. **Be Still:** Take a few moments of silence to listen. Sometimes, the Holy Spirit speaks in a still, small voice, and we need to quiet our hearts to hear Him.

3. **Pray Scripture:** Ask the Holy Spirit to reveal specific verses that align with what you're praying for. His Word is powerful and always accomplishes His purpose.

4. **Stay Sensitive:** Pay attention to the thoughts, impressions, or images that come to mind as you pray. These could be the Holy Spirit's way of directing your prayers.

5. **Trust Him:** Even if you don't understand why you're praying for something or someone, trust that the Holy Spirit knows exactly what is needed.

The Holy Spirit is our greatest ally in prayer. He not only equips us with the words to say but also fills us with the confidence to approach God boldly. Through Him, we experience the fullness of God's presence and power. As we yield to the Holy Spirit, our prayers become more than words—they become a powerful connection to the heart of God.

Let me leave you with this thought: The Holy Spirit is always with you, ready to intercede, guide, and empower your prayers. You are never alone in your prayer journey. Lean on Him, listen to His voice, and let Him transform your prayer life in ways you never thought possible.

CHAPTER 5

Trials, Tribulations, and Triumph

May I be honest? There have been times when life's trials felt overwhelming. I've faced multiple strokes, undergone multiple surgeries, and endured heart attacks that seemed unbearable. In those moments, I clung to prayer as my lifeline. I remember sitting in hospital rooms, tears streaming down my face, asking God, "Why is this happening?" The days felt long and heavy, but prayer became my refuge.

The Power of Prayer

One night, after one of my surgeries, I was so weak I could barely whisper. Yet, in that weakness, I felt the presence of God so strongly. It wasn't my strength that sustained me; it was His grace. I prayed, "Lord, I don't understand, but I trust You." And do you know what? He carried me through every moment. Each prayer I uttered, no matter how feeble, was met by His unwavering faithfulness. If there's one thing I've learned, it's this: God hears every cry, every sigh, and every whispered plea.

1 Peter 4:12-19 taught me that trials refine our faith. Peter writes, *"Do not be surprised at the fiery ordeal that has come on you to test you, as though something strange were happening to you. But rejoice inasmuch as you participate in the sufferings of Christ, so that you may be overjoyed when His glory is revealed."* Isn't that a beautiful reminder? Our trials are not meaningless; they have a purpose. They refine us,

strengthen us, and draw us closer to the One who sustains us.

Let me share another moment when prayer was my anchor. During one particularly dark season, I faced not only physical pain but also deep emotional wounds. It felt like everything I cared about was slipping through my fingers. Have you ever felt like that? Like no matter how hard you try, life keeps knocking you down? In that season, I learned to pray differently. Instead of asking God to take away the pain, I asked Him to use it. I said, "Lord, I don't know why this is happening, but I trust You. Teach me what You want me to learn and use this for Your glory."

And He did. Through that experience, I discovered a strength I didn't know I had—not my strength, but His. I also saw how my prayers began to change. They became less about my circumstances and more about His presence. I realized that even in the darkest valley, God is there, walking with us, holding us, and guiding us.

If you're in the middle of a trial right now, let me encourage you: you are not alone. The same God who carried me through countless storms is with you too. He sees your pain, He hears your prayers, and He is working—even when you can't see it. Psalm 34:18 says, "The Lord is close to the brokenhearted and saves those who are crushed in spirit." Hold on to that promise. God's closeness in our suffering is one of the most profound gifts of His love.

Prayer during trials isn't just about asking for relief; it's about trusting God's purpose. It's about believing that He can bring beauty from ashes and joy from mourning. One of the most powerful prayers we can pray in difficult times is, "Lord, I don't understand, but I trust You." That kind of faith moves the heart of God and opens the door for Him to work in ways we can't imagine.

I know it's not easy. There were days when I wanted to give up—days when the weight of the trial felt unbearable. But every time I turned to God in prayer, He met me with His peace, His strength, and His grace. And you know what? Looking back now, I can see how those struggles became testimonies of His faithfulness. Each trial I faced became an opportunity for God to show His power, His love, and His ability to redeem even the hardest circumstances.

Think of Job, who endured unimaginable suffering. He lost everything—his health, his wealth, and his family. Yet, in the midst of his pain, he declared, "Though He slay me, yet will I hope in Him" (Job 13:15). Job's story reminds us that our trials are not the end of the story. God is always at work, and His plans for us are good, even when we can't see them.

So, what trial are you facing right now? Is it a health issue, a broken relationship, financial struggles, or something else entirely? Whatever it is, I want to encourage you to bring it to God in prayer. Be honest with Him. Pour out your heart, your fears, and your frustrations. And then trust Him. Trust that He is with you, that He is for you, and that He will see you through.

As we close this chapter, I want to leave you with this: Trials are not the end; they are the beginning of God's work in us. Through prayer, we find the strength to endure, the faith to trust, and the hope to believe that God is making all things new. Hold on to Him, because He is holding on to you.

Chapter 6

Unleashing Heaven's Power

Have you ever wondered what happens when you pray? It's easy to picture prayer as a quiet moment between you and God, but the truth is, prayer unleashes the power of heaven. Behind the scenes, incredible spiritual activity occurs every time we pray. Daniel's story gives us a glimpse of this reality. In Daniel 10, we learn that from the moment he started praying, an angel was dispatched with an answer. Isn't that amazing? Yet, there was a delay because of spiritual warfare—a battle between heavenly forces and the forces of darkness.

This story has always fascinated me because it reminds us that prayer is not just a human activity; it's a spiritual act with far-reaching consequences. When we pray, we invite God to work in ways we cannot see. We might not always feel the effects immediately, but that doesn't mean nothing is happening. Just as Daniel's angel faced resistance from the "prince of Persia," our prayers often intersect with battles in the spiritual realm. Knowing this gives us a deeper understanding of why persistence in prayer is so important.

Let me share an example from my own life. There was a time when I was praying for a loved one who had turned away from God. For years, it seemed like nothing was changing. But I kept praying. I would ask God to soften their heart, to surround them with people who would point them back to Him, and to remove any barriers that stood in the way. I didn't see results right away, but I kept praying, trusting that God was working behind the scenes. Eventually, that loved one returned to faith, and when they shared their journey with me, I realized how God had been answering my prayers all along. Every prayer I had prayed had been like a drop of water, slowly but surely wearing away the hard surface of their heart.

Daniel's story teaches us that when we pray, angels are dispatched, battles are fought, and God's power is unleashed. Hebrews 1:14 says, "Are not all angels ministering spirits sent to serve those who will inherit salvation?" That means when you pray, you're not just speaking into the void; you're engaging the forces of heaven. Angels are sent to act on your behalf, whether it's to protect, guide, or carry out God's answers to your prayers.

But here's the thing: sometimes, the answer

doesn't come immediately. Like Daniel, we may have to wait. In those moments, it's easy to wonder if our prayers are even making a difference. Let me assure you—they are. The delay is not denial. It may be that God is orchestrating circumstances, preparing hearts, or, as in Daniel's case, engaging in spiritual warfare that requires time. Our job is to keep praying, to keep trusting, and to keep believing that God is at work.

One practical way to unleash heaven's power in your prayers is to pray Scripture. God's Word is powerful and always accomplishes His purposes. For example, when you're praying for protection, you can use Psalm 91:11: "For He will command His angels concerning you to guard you in all your ways." When you're praying for peace, you can declare Philippians 4:7: "And the peace of God, which transcends all understanding, will guard your hearts and your minds in Christ Jesus." Praying Scripture aligns your prayers with God's promises and invites His power into your situation.

Another key is to pray with boldness. Hebrews 4:16 encourages us to "approach God's throne of grace with confidence, so that we may receive mercy and find grace to help us in our time of need." Bold prayers are not about demanding from God; they're about trusting Him to do what only He can do. When we pray boldly, we acknowledge that God is able to do immeasurably more than we can ask or imagine (Ephesians 3:20).

I've seen the power of bold prayer firsthand. There was a situation where I was praying for a breakthrough in a ministry project. We faced obstacle after obstacle, and I felt tempted to give up. But instead, I began to pray boldly, asking God to remove every barrier and to make a way where there seemed to be no way. Within weeks, doors began to open, and the project moved forward in ways I could never have orchestrated on my own. It was a reminder that when we pray with faith and boldness, God delights in showing His power.

The Miracle in Greater Portmore

There are moments when God demonstrates His power through prayer in ways that are undeniable, immediate, and unforgettable. One such moment occurred during a Sunday morning service under the tent in Greater Portmore, St. Catherine, Jamaica.

The day started clear and sunny, with not a cloud in the sky. As the service was in full swing, a sudden whirlwind stirred up the football field across from the tent, lifting a massive cloud of dust that enveloped the congregation. The dust was so thick that it became difficult to breathe. With no other recourse, I lifted my eyes to the heavens and prayed, "Lord, please send rain." Before I could finish my prayer, raindrops began to fall. The rain poured down with such intensity that the tent began to flood, and its poles started to loosen. It seemed inevitable that the structure would collapse on us.

In that moment of desperation, I prayed again, "Lord, thank You for the rain, but please hold it now, or this tent will fall on us." Before I could finish speaking, the rain stopped, as though commanded by God Himself. The air cleared, the tent stood firm, and we were left in awe of the immediacy and power of prayer. It was a vivid reminder that God hears and responds to His people.

This extraordinary experience underscores the truth that prayer is not merely an act of faith; it is a demonstration of the power of a living, present, and attentive God. Just as Daniel's prayers in Chapter 10 of his book unleashed angelic activity, our prayers today carry the same weight and significance in the spiritual realm. When we cry out to God in faith, heaven moves on our behalf.

Finally, don't underestimate the power of collective prayer. When believers come together to pray, the impact is multiplied. Jesus said in Matthew 18:19-20, "Again, truly I tell you that if two of you on earth agree about anything they ask for, it will be done for them by my Father in heaven. For where two or three gather in My name, there am I with them." There is strength in numbers, and when we join our voices in prayer, we unleash heaven's power in an even greater way.

As we close this chapter, I want to encourage you: never underestimate the impact of your prayers. Whether you're praying for a loved one, a personal need, or a global issue, know that your prayers are heard, and they make a difference. You are partnering with God to bring His kingdom to earth, and there is no greater privilege. So keep praying, keep trusting, and keep unleashing heaven's power through the incredible gift of prayer.

Chapter 7

Persistent Prayer

Let's talk about persistence in prayer, one of the most powerful yet challenging aspects of our faith journey. Jesus illustrated this beautifully in the parable of the persistent widow found in Luke 18:1-7. The widow, faced with injustice, continuously pleaded her case to an unjust judge. Despite his initial resistance, her unwavering determination moved him to act on her behalf. Jesus used this example to teach us a vital truth: we should always pray and never give up. Unlike the unjust judge, our Heavenly Father is loving, faithful, and just, eager to respond to the cries of His children.

Persistence in prayer is not just a biblical principle; it is a reflection of our faith and trust in God. There have been countless moments in my life when I've struggled to keep praying for something that seemed impossible. Perhaps you've felt the same—praying for a breakthrough, a loved one's salvation, or guidance in a tough situation, only to feel like your prayers were hitting a wall. But here's the truth: persistent prayer is an act of faith. It is a declaration that we trust in God's timing, His wisdom, and His sovereign plan, even when the answers seem delayed.

Let me share a story close to my heart. There was a season in my life when I fervently prayed for a family member to come to know Christ. Day after day, year after year, I lifted their name to heaven, yet there were no visible signs of change. At times, discouragement crept in, and I questioned whether my prayers were making any difference. But every time I thought about giving up, the Holy Spirit reminded me of Luke 18:1: "Then Jesus told his disciples a parable to show them that they should always pray and not give up." Those words reignited my faith and gave me the courage to keep praying.

Finally, after what felt like an eternity, God answered in a way that only He could. That family member had a powerful encounter with the Lord, leading to their transformation and salvation. It was a moment that reminded me of the faithfulness of God and the importance of persistent prayer. Those years of waiting weren't wasted—they were a time of preparation, both for them and for me.

But why does God ask us to persist in prayer? Is

He reluctant to act? Does He need convincing? Absolutely not. Persistence in prayer isn't about changing God's mind; it's about transforming our hearts. Through persistence, we learn to trust Him more deeply, to depend on His strength, and to align our desires with His will. Sometimes, the waiting season is God's way of preparing us for the answer. He may be working behind the scenes, orchestrating circumstances or refining our character to fully receive what we're asking for.

Consider the story of Daniel. In Daniel 10, we see him praying and fasting for 21 days, seeking understanding from God. Unknown to Daniel, from the moment he began praying, God sent an angel with the answer. However, spiritual warfare delayed the angel's arrival. What if Daniel had stopped praying on day 15 or 20? While the Bible doesn't explicitly answer this question, it's clear that persistent prayer is crucial in the spiritual realm. It is through persistence that we partner with God to see His will accomplished.

Here are some practical steps to help you persist in prayer:

1. **Set a Regular Time for Prayer:** Create a consistent routine for prayer. Whether it's early in the morning, during a quiet lunch break, or at the end of your day, setting aside intentional time to connect with God builds the foundation for a thriving prayer life.

2. **Keep a Prayer Journal:** Document your prayer requests and record how God answers them. Revisiting past answered prayers will strengthen your faith and remind you of His faithfulness during seasons of waiting.

3. **Pray with Others:** Join a prayer group or find a prayer partner. There's immense power in united prayer. As Jesus said, "For where two or three gather in my name, there am I with them" (Matthew 18:20).

4. **Use Scripture in Prayer:** God's Word is alive and powerful, and praying His promises can fuel your persistence. For example, remind yourself of Jeremiah 29:12: "Then you will call on me and come and pray to me, and I will listen to you."

5. **Be Honest with God:** Don't hide your struggles. Share your doubts, frustrations, and fears with Him. Ask for renewed strength and faith to continue praying. As Paul reminds us, "Do not be anxious about anything, but in every situation, by prayer and petition, with thanksgiving, present

your requests to God" (Philippians 4:6).

6. **Celebrate Small Victories:** Sometimes, answers come in stages. Celebrate the small signs of progress and thank God for them. These moments remind us that He is working, even if we don't see the full picture yet.

Persistent prayer is not about pestering God; it's about partnering with Him. Every prayer we lift to heaven is a seed planted in faith, and in due time, it will bear fruit. As Galatians 6:9 encourages us, "Let us not become weary in doing good, for at the proper time we will reap a harvest if we do not give up."

So, my dear friend, keep praying. Keep believing. And trust that the God who hears every whisper, every cry, and every plea is working all things together for good. Your persistence in prayer

The Power of Prayer

is never wasted—it is an act of faith that moves the heart of God and invites His power into your life.

Chapter 8

Practical Prayers for Everyday Life

Prayer doesn't have to be complicated. In fact, some of the most meaningful prayers happen in the simplest moments of our daily lives. It's easy to fall into the mindset that prayer needs to be formal, lengthy, or performed in a specific setting to be effective. But the beauty of prayer is its accessibility. God invites us to talk with Him anywhere, anytime, about anything. Whether it's a heartfelt cry in a moment of crisis or a quiet whisper of gratitude during a busy day, every prayer matters to Him.

One of the most liberating truths about prayer is that it can be woven into the fabric of our daily routines. I often find myself praying while washing dishes, walking, or driving. Those prayers may not be part of a formal "quiet time," but they are just as precious to God. What about you? Have you ever whispered a prayer while waiting in line, asked for wisdom before a meeting, or sought peace during a stressful moment? These prayers remind us that God is present in every detail of our lives, and they invite Him to walk with us through each moment.

The Bible beautifully captures this kind of prayerful living in 1 Thessalonians 5:16-18: "Rejoice always, pray without ceasing, give thanks in all circumstances; for this is the will of God in Christ Jesus for you." Praying without ceasing doesn't mean we're on our knees 24/7—it means cultivating a constant awareness of God's presence and inviting Him into every part of our day. It's about living with an open line of communication with our Heavenly Father, where prayer becomes as natural as breathing.

Let me share a personal story. There was a season in my life when I felt completely overwhelmed by the demands of ministry, family, and personal responsibilities. My to-do list seemed endless, and I didn't know where to start. One morning, as I stared at my list with a sense of dread, I paused and prayed, "Lord, give me wisdom to prioritize what matters most today. Help me not to get lost in busyness but to see where You want me to focus." That simple prayer shifted my perspective. Suddenly, the overwhelming chaos felt manageable. I approached my day with clarity and peace, knowing that God was guiding my steps. It was a powerful reminder that God cares about every detail of our lives—even the small things like organizing a schedule.

One of the most impactful forms of prayer is intercession—praying on behalf of others. Have you ever had someone ask, "Will you pray for me?" and then felt unsure how or when to do it? Here's a practice I've adopted: whenever someone asks for prayer, I stop and pray for them immediately, even if it's a quick, silent prayer. It's a simple yet powerful way to demonstrate love and faith in action. Intercessory prayer reminds us that we are part of a larger body of believers, standing in the gap for one another and lifting each other's burdens to God.

Another way to deepen your prayer life is by praying Scripture. God's Word is filled with promises and truths that can guide our prayers and anchor our faith. For example, when I feel anxious, I often pray Philippians 4:6-7: "Lord, You tell me not to be anxious about anything, but to bring everything to You in prayer with thanksgiving. Right now, I bring this situation to You, trusting that Your peace, which transcends all understanding, will guard my heart and mind." Praying Scripture not only reminds us of God's faithfulness but also aligns our hearts with His will.

Here are some practical tips for making prayer an integral part of your daily life:

1. **Start Your Day with Prayer**: Dedicate the first few moments of your day to God. Thank Him for a new day, ask for His guidance, and invite Him to walk with you through whatever lies ahead.

2. **Incorporate Breath Prayers**: These are short, simple prayers you can say in a single

breath, such as "Jesus, give me peace" or "Lord, guide me today." They're perfect for moments when you need a quick connection with God.

3. **Keep a Gratitude Journal**: At the end of each day, write down three things you're thankful for. Gratitude shifts our focus from what's wrong to what's right and strengthens our relationship with God.

4. **Use Prayer Prompts**: Set reminders on your phone or place sticky notes in your home or workspace with simple prompts like "Pray for wisdom" or "Thank God for today."

5. **Turn Chores into Prayer Time**: Use everyday tasks like washing dishes, folding laundry, or walking the dog as opportunities to talk with God. These moments can

become sacred when we invite Him into them.

6. **Pray as a Family**: Involve your family in prayer during meals or bedtime. Take turns thanking God for specific blessings and praying for the needs on your hearts. These shared moments can strengthen your family's bond and deepen your collective faith.

What I love most about practical, everyday prayers is that they remind us of God's nearness. He's not only present in church or during our designated prayer times; He's with us in the ordinary and mundane moments of life. As Psalm 145:18 declares, "The Lord is near to all who call on Him, to all who call on Him in truth." When we invite Him into our day, we open the door for His peace, wisdom, and joy to transform even the most routine tasks.

Remember, prayer isn't about perfection—it's about connection. God doesn't measure the worth of your prayers by their length or eloquence. He cherishes every word you speak to Him, whether it's a desperate cry for help or a simple "thank You."

So, let's make prayer a natural part of our everyday lives. Let's talk to God as we move through our routines, listen for His voice in the busyness, and trust that He cares about every detail. Even if you start with just a few moments each day, you'll discover the incredible ways God meets you in those simple yet sacred moments.

Chapter 9

Prayer as Active Ministry

Prayer isn't passive; it's powerful. It is a ministry in its own right—one that any believer can engage in regardless of their age, circumstances, or physical abilities. When I first heard the PUSH acronym—Pray Until Something Happens—it struck a chord with me. Prayer requires persistence, patience, and bold faith, but the results are worth every moment spent on our knees. Through prayer, we become active participants in God's work, advancing His kingdom and impacting the world around us.

The Power of Prayer

Have you ever felt the Holy Spirit prompting you to pray for someone or a situation? I remember a time when I woke up in the middle of the night with an unexplainable burden to pray for a friend. I didn't know why, but I obeyed. Later, I learned that at that exact moment, my friend had been facing a critical decision and felt an overwhelming sense of peace and clarity. That's the power of prayer—it reaches beyond our understanding and aligns us with God's purpose.

Jesus Himself modeled this kind of active ministry. Throughout the Gospels, we see Him taking time to pray, often withdrawing to solitary places to commune with the Father. In John 17, Jesus prays for His disciples and for all believers, demonstrating the importance of interceding for others. If Jesus, the Son of God, prioritized prayer, how much more should we?

Prayer as active ministry means stepping into the gap for others. Ezekiel 22:30 says, "I looked for someone among them who would build up the wall and stand before me in the gap on behalf of the land so I would not have to destroy it, but I found no one." This verse reminds us that God seeks people who will stand in the gap through prayer. When we intercede, we are partnering with God to bring His will to earth.

Think of Moses, who interceded for the Israelites after they sinned by worshiping the golden calf. His prayers moved God's heart and spared the people from destruction (Exodus 32:11-14). Or consider Esther, who fasted and prayed before approaching King Xerxes to save her people. Her prayers and bold action changed the course of history. These stories remind us that prayer is not passive; it's a dynamic, active ministry that has the power to shift circumstances and bring about God's purposes.

In my own life, I've seen the ripple effects of prayer as active ministry. There was a time when my church was struggling to grow. Attendance was declining, and morale was low. A small group of us decided to commit to prayer, meeting every week to seek God's guidance and blessings. We prayed for the church's leadership, for the congregation, and for our community. Slowly but surely, things began to change. New families started attending, ministries were revitalized, and a sense of unity and excitement returned. It wasn't our efforts that brought about the change—it was God responding to our prayers.

Active prayer also equips us for spiritual warfare. Ephesians 6:12 reminds us that "our struggle is not against flesh and blood, but against the rulers, against the authorities, against the powers of this dark world and against the spiritual forces of evil in the heavenly realms." Prayer is our weapon in this battle. When we pray, we take a stand against darkness, declaring God's authority and inviting His light to prevail.

Here are some practical ways to make prayer an active ministry in your life:

1. Pray with Purpose: Before you begin praying, ask the Holy Spirit to guide your thoughts and focus your prayers. Consider writing down specific requests or areas of concern.

2. Intercede for Others: Create a list of people and situations to pray for regularly. Whether it's a family member, a friend, or a global issue, your prayers make a difference.

3. Pray Boldly: Don't be afraid to ask God for big things. He is able to do immeasurably more than we can ask or imagine (Ephesians 3:20).

4. Join a Prayer Group: Partnering with others in prayer multiplies its impact. Find a group at your church or start one with friends.

5. Pray for the Nations: Expand your prayers beyond your immediate circle. Pray for missionaries, persecuted Christians, and world leaders.

6. 6. Fast and Pray: Fasting amplifies the power of prayer by helping us focus more fully on God and His will.

As we engage in prayer as active ministry, we must also trust God with the results. Sometimes, the answers don't come in the way or timeframe we expect. But we can rest in the assurance that God is working all things together for good (Romans 8:28). Our role is to pray faithfully and leave the outcomes in His hands.

Prayer is one of the most impactful ways we can serve others and advance God's kingdom. It's not just a personal practice; it's a ministry that reaches into the lives of those around us and beyond. When we pray, we are co-laboring with God, bringing heaven to earth and aligning ourselves with His plans.

Let me leave you with this thought: Every prayer you pray is a seed planted in faith. Some seeds sprout quickly, while others take time to grow, but none are wasted. As you commit to prayer as active ministry, you will see God move in ways you never imagined. So keep praying, keep trusting, and keep partnering with Him to make an eternal impact.

CHAPTER 10

Living a Life of Prayer

What does it mean to live a life of prayer? For some, the idea might sound daunting—a constant, unending conversation with God? How do we make that practical? For me, it's about seeing prayer as more than just a moment—it's a lifestyle. It's not about finding perfection in how we pray; it's about building a relationship with God that flows into every part of our day, guiding our thoughts, decisions, and actions.

There was a time when I thought prayer was

something I had to schedule into my life. And while setting aside specific times for prayer is important, I realized that prayer can become a rhythm, much like breathing. It's about inviting God into every moment of my life—whether I'm standing at the pulpit delivering a sermon, preparing a meal, or simply sitting quietly at the end of a long day.

The apostle Paul encourages us in 1 Thessalonians 5:17 to "pray without ceasing." At first glance, that sounds impossible. But what Paul is really inviting us into is a mindset of prayer—a heart posture that remains connected to God throughout the day. It's an ongoing awareness that He is with us in every moment and that we can turn to Him anytime, anywhere.

Prayer as a Lifestyle

Living a life of prayer doesn't mean abandoning your daily responsibilities to sit in a quiet room all day. It means weaving prayer into the fabric of your life. When I'm driving, I'll often pray for the people in the cars around me, asking God to bless them and keep them safe. When I'm grocery shopping, I might thank God for the ability to provide for my family. And when I'm meeting with someone who's struggling, I silently ask God to give me wisdom and the right words to say.

Living a life of prayer also means being intentional about listening to God. So often, our prayers can become one-sided conversations where we do all the talking. But prayer is a dialogue, not a monologue. Taking time to pause, to listen, and to be still allows us to hear God's gentle whispers. Psalm 46:10 reminds us, "Be still, and know that I am God." In the stillness, we often find His guidance, His reassurance, and His peace.

The Impact of a Prayerful Life

A life of prayer transforms not only us but also those around us. When we live in constant communion with God, His love, peace, and joy naturally overflow into our interactions with others. Have you ever met someone who exudes a quiet confidence and calm no matter what they're going through? Chances are, they've cultivated a lifestyle of prayer.

I remember visiting a dear friend who had been battling a serious illness for years. Despite her physical pain, she radiated a peace that was almost tangible. When I asked her how she remained so strong, she simply said, "I talk to Jesus all day long. He's my strength." Her life was a testament to the power of prayer—not just as an occasional act, but as a way of life.

Practical Ways to Live a Life of Prayer

Here are a few simple ways you can integrate prayer into your everyday life:

1. Begin and End Your Day with Prayer: Start your morning by dedicating your day to God. At night, reflect on His faithfulness and thank Him for the blessings you experienced.

2. Pray as You Go: Turn everyday activities into opportunities for prayer. Whether you're walking the dog, folding laundry, or waiting in line, use those moments to talk to God.

3. Set Reminders: Place sticky notes with prayer prompts around your home or set alarms on your phone to remind you to pause and pray throughout the day.

4. Pray for Others: When someone shares a need with you, take a moment to pray for them right then and there. You'll not only bless them but also strengthen your own faith.

5. Create a Prayer Space: Designate a quiet corner in your home where you can retreat for focused prayer. Fill it with items that inspire you, like your Bible, a journal, or a candle.

6. Incorporate Gratitude: Make it a habit to thank God for the small and big blessings in your life. Gratitude transforms our perspective and keeps our hearts aligned with His.

Encouragement for the Journey

Living a life of prayer is not about achieving

perfection; it's about walking in step with God. Some days, your prayers may feel vibrant and full of faith. Other days, they may be as simple as, "Lord, help me." And that's okay. God isn't looking for polished prayers; He's looking for your heart.

As you commit to a life of prayer, you'll find that it becomes second nature. You'll begin to see God's hand in the details of your life, and your trust in Him will deepen. You'll also become more attuned to His voice, recognizing His guidance in ways you never did before. Let's encourage each other to make prayer a lifestyle. Let's commit to walking in constant communion with God, reflecting His love and power in a world that desperately needs Him. When we live a life of prayer, we become beacons of His light, pointing others to the hope and peace found in Him.

Conclusion

The power of prayer is truly limitless, a gift available to all who believe and trust in the Lord. Prayer is the sacred bridge that connects our hearts to His, allowing us to access the fullness of His presence, power, and unfailing love. It is through prayer that we are invited to commune with the Creator of the universe, to pour out our hearts before Him, and to receive His divine guidance, peace, and strength.

As we've journeyed through the pages of this book, we've explored the many facets of prayer—its principles, its persistence, and its potential to transform lives. Prayer is not merely a ritual or a duty; it is a relationship. It is the heart's cry of a child reaching out to a loving Father, confident that He hears and responds. James 5:16 reminds us, "The prayer of a righteous person is powerful and effective." This promise assures us that every prayer, offered in faith, has the power to bring about real change—not only in our circumstances but also within our hearts.

Life will inevitably bring storms, challenges, and uncertainties. Yet, prayer becomes our anchor in those moments of turbulence, grounding us in the unshakable hope of God's promises. Philippians 4:6-7 encourages us, "Do not be anxious about anything, but in every situation, by prayer and petition, with thanksgiving, present your requests to God. And the peace of God, which transcends all understanding, will guard your hearts and your minds in Christ Jesus." When we bring our worries to God in prayer, He replaces our anxiety with a peace that defies explanation—a peace rooted in His presence.

Prayer is not confined to specific times, places, or circumstances. It is a living, breathing conversation with God that can happen anywhere—whether whispered in the stillness of dawn, lifted in the chaos of a busy day, or cried out in the depths of despair. Every prayer matters to God. Psalm 34:17 assures us, "The righteous cry out, and the Lord hears them; He delivers them from all their troubles." In His perfect timing, God answers our prayers in ways that align with His will and our ultimate good.

As you close this book, my prayer for you is that you would be inspired to embrace a life of prayer with renewed passion and faith. Trust God with your deepest fears and desires, intercede for others with compassion, and walk daily in communion with Him. Remember, no prayer is too small, no request too impossible, and no moment too ordinary to invite God into.

Let prayer become the rhythm of your life. Let it shape your thoughts, guide your actions, and draw you ever closer to the heart of God. Just as the prelude spoke of a heavenly spark, may prayer light the path ahead of you, igniting faith, hope, and love in ways you never imagined. Together, let's continue to pray, believe, and marvel as God's power is revealed through the simple yet profound act of prayer. So, keep praying. Keep believing. And together, let's marvel as God's power is revealed through the simple yet profound act of prayer. As Hebrews 4:16 encourages us, "Let us then approach God's throne of grace with confidence, so that we may receive mercy and find grace to help us in our time of need." Amen.

A Prayer About Prayer

Heavenly Father,

Thank You for the incredible gift of prayer—a sacred space where we can meet You, where our hearts can be heard, and where our burdens can be laid at Your feet. Sometimes, Lord, we take this gift for granted or we struggle to find the words, yet You remind us that even when we don't know how to pray, Your Spirit intercedes for us with groans too deep for words. Thank You for always meeting us where we are, whether we come in joy, in sorrow, in gratitude, or in desperation.

Lord, teach us how to pray. Not just with words, but with hearts that are fully surrendered to You.

The Power of Prayer

Help us to approach You with faith that moves mountains and trust that rests in Your timing, even when answers seem delayed. Remind us, Father, that prayer is not just about changing our circumstances but about changing us—aligning our will with Yours and transforming us from the inside out.

God, forgive us for the times we've treated prayer as an afterthought or a checklist item. Help us to see it for what it truly is: a lifeline, a privilege, a divine invitation to commune with You. Stir in us a desire to pray persistently, not because You need to be convinced, but because You long for a deeper relationship with us. Help us to pray boldly, knowing that You are able to do immeasurably more than all we ask or imagine.

Father, we pray for a renewed passion for prayer—not as a duty, but as a joy. May we pray not only for ourselves but for others—for our families, our communities, and our world. Teach us to intercede with love, to listen with patience, and to trust that even when we don't see immediate results, You are working behind the scenes in ways we cannot fathom. Lord, help us to pray in every season of life—in the mundane and the miraculous, in the valleys and on the mountaintops. May we come to You with childlike faith, trusting that You hear every whisper and treasure every word. Remind us that prayer is not about perfection, but connection.

Thank You for being a God who listens, a God who cares, and a God who answers according to Your perfect will. Let prayer become the rhythm of our lives, a constant thread that ties us to You. May it draw us closer to Your heart, deepen our faith, and inspire us to live lives that reflect Your love. We love You, Lord, and we thank You for the gift of prayer. May our lives be a continual offering of praise and communion with You. In precious name of Jesus'.

Amen.

Dr. Letitia McPherson

On sale on Amazon, Barns and Noble
and at www.gracebookstore.com

By God's Grace I Stand
The Power of Forgiveness
The Power of Faith
From the Mouth of the Prophet
Facing the Storms of Life
Walking Through the Valley
The Potter, The Clay, the Process

PLACES TO FIND ME

The Power of Prayer

Join my mailing list for news, contests and exclusive content

Email me - bygodsgrace@bygodsgraceistand.com.

Find me on Facebook -
https://www.facebook.com/bishop.mcpherson *
https://www.facebook.com/godsgraceistand

Websites: https://www.bygodsgraceistand.com
https://www.gracebookstore.com

My author page -
https://www.facebook.com/Autho.rmcpherson

https://www.amazon.ca *
https://www.amazon.ca - Kindle Edition.

www.ingramcontent.com/pod-product-compliance
Lightning Source LLC
Chambersburg PA
CBHW050244170426
43202CB00015B/2914